THE TRUTH
ABOUT ANGELS

DR. DAVID JEREMIAH

MULTNOMAH BOOKS • SISTERS, OREGON

THE TRUTH ABOUT ANGELS
Highlights from *What the Bible Says about Angels*
published by Multnomah Books
a part of the Questar publishing family
© 1996 by David Jeremiah

International Standard Book Number: 0-88070-1-57673-027-1

Cover design by David Uttley
Cover illustration by Douglas Klauba
Printed in the United States of America

Most Scripture quotations are from: *The Holy Bible, New International Version* (NIV) © 1973, 1984
by International Bible Society, used by permission of Zondervan Publishing House

98 99 00 01 02 03 — 10 9 8 7 6 5 4

*All glory be
to the God of the angels*

Part One

MYSTERIOUS PRESENCE

For I am convinced that neither death nor life,
neither angels nor demons . . . nor any powers . . .
will be able to separate us from the love of God
that is in Christ Jesus our Lord.

———

ROMANS 8:38-39

There's a lot more to this "strange" topic of angels than we imagine. Once we honestly investigate the amazing things Scripture tells us about them, we actually find ourselves drawn closer to God, instead of being distracted and turned away from him. Anyone who goes into a study of angels with a high view of God will come away with an even higher view.

. . .for Satan himself masquerades as an angel of light.

———————

2 CORINTHIANS 11:14

A stronger belief in angels is no guarantee of greater understanding of God's truth. The devil can ensnare us as much through "angelism" as he can through materialism or sexual lust or power-hunger. In fact he has scored some of his greatest triumphs in the disguise of angels.

"If you are the Son of God," he said,
"throw yourself down. For it is written:
'He will command his angels concerning you,
and they will lift you up in their hands, so that you
will not strike your foot against a stone.' "

————

MATTHEW 4:6

The Bible gives no indication angels will respond if we pray directly to them for help. In fact in Scripture we don't find any instances of people even asking God to send them an angel's protection. And the only person in Scripture who tried persuading someone else to seek help from an angel was Satan, who quoted an Old Testament verse about angelic protection while tempting Jesus in the wilderness.

I saw the Lord sitting on his throne
with all the host of heaven standing around him
on his right and on his left.

———————

1 KINGS 22:19

I t looks as if angels will be a big part of our eternal environment, which will be far more substantial than our short and shadowy presence on this earth. Being eternal themselves, angels have a greater claim to "reality" than our homes and jobs and hobbies. And unlike our homes and jobs and hobbies, the holy angels are always pointing us in the right direction: toward God.

Are not all angels ministering spirits sent to serve those who will inherit salvation?

HEBREWS 1:14

WHO are these people destined to "inherit salvation"? The Bible makes it clear that this refers only to those who come to know Christ as Savior. It's to serve only them that angels are sent. If someone claims to have seen an angel yet that person professes no allegiance to Jesus Christ, it's likely that any angel he saw (if he truly saw one at all) was a fallen one — one of the devil's messengers, not the Lord's. Not every angel is from God.

Whom have I in heaven but you?
And earth has nothing I desire besides you.

PSALM 73:25

We ought to try to know as much about angels as God has determined to reveal to us — and then be content to leave it at that. Someday we'll understand more. But try crossing that line now and you can end up doing yourself damage…. Besides God there is no one on earth and no one in heaven — not even angels — who can give your soul true fulfillment.

The Sadducees say . . .
that there are neither angels nor spirits . . ..

———————

ACTS 23:8

Those who have doubts might run the risk of suffering the same fate as the Sadducees, the only group of folks identified in the Bible as not believing in angels…. The Sadducees disappeared from history without a trace before the first century ended, though in Jesus' day they were Israel's most powerful Jews.

*The Spirit clearly says that in later times
some will abandon the faith and follow
deceiving spirits and things taught by demons.*

———————

1 TIMOTHY 4:1

ost Christians agree demonic activity will increase as we near the last days. We have seen and will probably continue to see greater attacks from the forces of spiritual evil. So I ask you: Isn't it reasonable to expect that as demonic activity increases while we near the day of the Lord's return, angelic activity will also increase? It makes sense.

In speaking of the angels he says,
"He makes his angels winds,
his servants flames of fire."

———————

HEBREWS 1:7

We must not create or reshape angels according to our own fancy. Countless multitudes have fallen into this error. In today's spiritual smorgasbord an angel can be anything you make it out to be. A majority of the angel representations we see — in paintings and giftbooks, or as lapel pins and china figurines, or gracing a host of other varieties of merchandise — are merely the product of human imagination.

As the deer pants for streams of water,
so my soul pants for you, O God.

———————

PSALM 42:1

We must never let angels replace God in our lives. This is a giant snare today for those who don't understand Scripture's teaching. I'm convinced that spiritual fads and tangents like those we see in angelmania are a tool of the enemy to keep us from following hard after God.

Then the Lord said . . . "I will send an angel
before you . . . . But I will not go with you,
because you are a stiff-necked people
and I might destroy you on the way."

———

EXODUS 33:1-3

The very thought that we would have an angel's help *instead of God's* should fill us with grief, as it once did to the people of Israel.... Did the Israelites jump for joy when they heard about this change in leadership for the journey? Did they consider an angel a more companionable guide than God? No. "When the people heard these distressing words, they began to mourn...."

Who is like the Lord our God,
the One who sits enthroned on high,
who stoops down to look on the heavens . . . ?

———————

PSALM 113:5-6

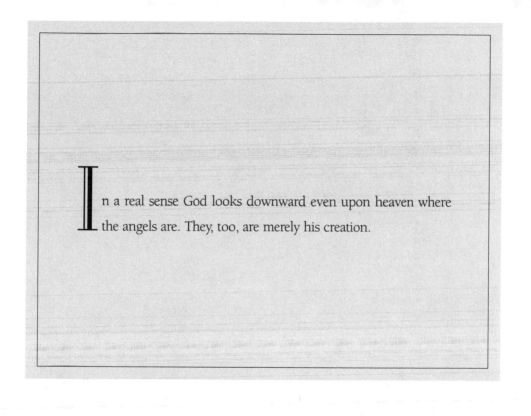

In a real sense God looks downward even upon heaven where the angels are. They, too, are merely his creation.

Let us be thankful,
and so worship God acceptably
with reverence and awe,
for our God is a consuming fire.

———————

HEBREWS 12:28-29

ystery saturates this whole topic. But mystery is good and healthy for us, and maybe more now than ever. So many Christians today are lacking in awe and a sense of mystery when they consider the things of God. My prayer is that this presumption will start to be corrected as we gain respect for the secrets surrounding God's angels.

The Lord answered Job . . .
"Where were you when I laid the earth's foundation . . .
while the morning stars sang together
and all the angels shouted for joy?"

———————

JOB 38:1-7

The Lord told Job that angels were already on the scene to celebrate when the earth was created. Job wasn't there when the earth was formed, but the angels were, and having a good time of it too. Very likely the angels are older than anything in the world as we see it.

At the resurrection
people will neither marry nor be given in marriage;
they will be like the angels in heaven.

———————

MATTHEW 22:30

Has God created any more angels since then? I have no biblical reason to believe he has. And apparently there's been no reduction in their number either. Nor has there been any increase, since angels don't reproduce — according to Jesus' statement that angels don't marry.

You have come to thousands upon thousands of angels in joyful assembly.

HEBREWS 12:22

We have as many angels today as we've ever had. And exactly how many angels is that? No precise count is given in Scripture, but there's plenty of evidence that they make up a mighty multitude.

*I tell you that their angels in heaven
always see the face of my Father in heaven.*

———————

MATTHEW 18:10

eaven is their dwelling place because angels belong exclusively to God. The best definition of heaven is that it's God's dwelling place. "Heaven is my throne," God says, and that is where angels work and live. They inhabit the throne-room of God, because they belong to God.

I tell you,
whoever acknowledges me before men,
the Son of Man will also acknowledge him
before the angels of God. But he who disowns me
before men will be disowned
before the angels of God.

———

LUKE 12:8-9

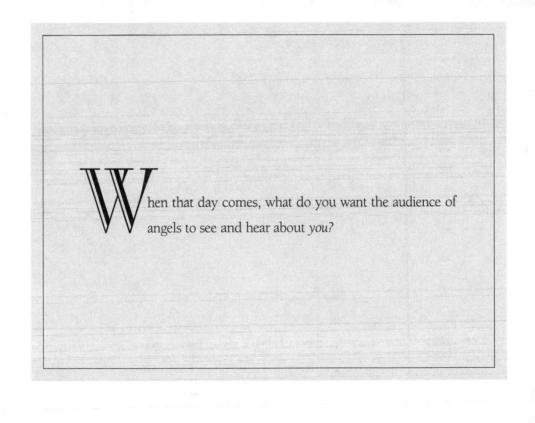

When that day comes, what do you want the audience of
angels to see and hear about *you?*

Then I looked and
heard the voice of many angels,
numbering thousands upon thousands,
and ten thousand times ten thousand.
They encircled the throne . . . .

———————

REVELATION 5:11

Angels are real, but without material substance as we think of it. They apparently have no physical nature, no breath or blood. If they occupy some form of permanent bodies, these would be spiritual bodies, perhaps like the ones we'll wear someday in eternity. It must be their spiritual nature — as well as their spiritual holiness — that allows angels the continual proximity to God they enjoy, for in this they are like God.

For who in the skies above
can compare with the Lord?
Who is like the Lord
among the heavenly beings?

———

PSALM 89:6

In their spiritual state, angels have many limitations that God can never have. For example, angels cannot be in more than one place at once, unlike God, who is everywhere at once. Only God is infinite in his whereabouts; he is omnipresent.

In the council of the holy ones
God is greatly feared;
he is more awesome
than all who surround him.

———————

PSALM 89:7

Angels are also limited in knowledge. Jesus said the angels don't know the time of his second coming to the world. But God in heaven always knows the end from the beginning, and can communicate his plans to whomever he chooses. He is omniscient, all-knowing, infinite in knowledge.

The mystery of the seven stars . . . is this:
The seven stars are the angels
of the seven churches.

———————

REVELATION 1:20

Since Scripture sometimes associates angels with stars, is all this a hint that the substance of angels is more like that of stars — orbs of fire — than anything else? It could be that even the miraculous star that brought the wise men to Bethlehem was in actuality an angel, faithfully serving God in his appointed task of guiding worshipers to the newborn King.

Then I saw another mighty angel coming down
from heaven. He was robed in a cloud,
with a rainbow above his head;
his face was like the sun,
and his legs were like fiery pillars.

REVELATION 10:1

It appears to be this particular aspect of angelic demeanor —their shining brilliance — that Satan tries to counterfeit. For Paul warns us that "Satan himself masquerades as an angel of light." But whatever the glow surrounding angels, it comes straight from the light of God. Only God's holy angels are truly "angels of light."

Do not forget to entertain strangers,
for by so doing some people have
entertained angels without knowing it.

———————

HEBREWS 13:2

If you really believe in angels and would enjoy entertaining or honoring them (as a thank-you gesture perhaps for everything they do for you), consider improving your hospitality to strangers. Not until eternity will you know if any of them were angels, but the possibility anyway is exciting.

An angel of the Lord appeared to him in a dream
and said, "Joseph son of David, do not be afraid
to take Mary home as your wife. . . ."
When Joseph woke up, he did what the angel
of the Lord had commanded him
and took Mary home as his wife.

———————

MATTHEW 1:20-24

The New Testament story of Joseph the husband of Mary contains the most dream appearances by angels in the Scriptures. It also contains some of the strongest examples of obedience. Joseph didn't get into angelmania from all of his supernatural experiences. He just did what God's angel told him to do.

If I speak in the tongues of men and of angels,
but have not love, I am only a resounding gong
or a clanging cymbal.

———————

1 CORINTHIANS 13:1

ngels apparently have their own spiritual languages, though 1 Corinthians 13 makes it clear that these "tongues of angels" are not as important or as beautiful in God's eyes as the simple human language of our love in action.

*Those who are considered worthy of taking part
in that age and in the resurrection from the dead . . .
can no longer die; for they are like the angels.
They are God's children,
since they are children of the resurrection.*

LUKE 20:35-36

As spiritual beings, angels know nothing of what it's like to get ill, grow old, and eventually die. Someday we, too, will be beyond the reach of those afflictions. We and the angels will share permanent citizenship in God's heavenly kingdom forever.

Part Two

POWERFUL
GUARDIANS

So the Lord God banished him from
the Garden of Eden. . . . After he drove the man out,
he placed on the east side of the Garden of Eden
cherubim and a flaming sword flashing back
and forth to guard the way to the tree of life.

GENESIS 3:24

It's by no means a peaceful, pleasant scene. What catches our attention first is a flaming sword flashing back and forth. These heavenly beings are armed soldiers placed here by the Holy God because his holy creation has just been contaminated by the sin of Adam and Eve. The soldiers' mission: "to guard the way to the tree of life." We can tell they mean business.

And the Lord sent an angel,
who annihilated all the fighting men
and the leaders and officers in the camp
of the Assyrian king.

———

2 CHRONICLES 32:21

ivorced from any credibility forever are the thoughts of plump baby "cherubs" or pale ladies with see-through wings traced in glitter across our Christmas cards. No, real angels have been and are and shall forever be awesome warriors for God, agents of his wrath and power.

This is what the Lord says—
Israel's King and Redeemer,
the Lord of Hosts:
I am the first and I am the last. . . .

ISAIAH 44:6

More than 250 times in the Bible, God calls himself "the Lord of Hosts," meaning "the Lord of Heavenly Armies." It's as if God wants us to envision those robust ranks of troops whenever we hear him called by that name.

For he will
command his angels concerning you
to guard you in all your ways.

———

PSALM 91:11

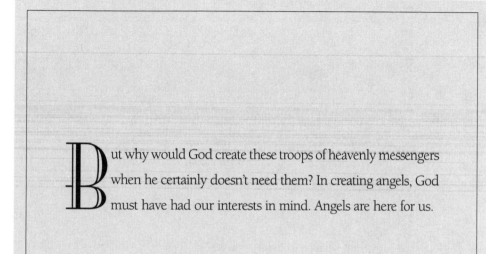

ut why would God create these troops of heavenly messengers when he certainly doesn't need them? In creating angels, God must have had our interests in mind. Angels are here for us.

And the four angels who had been kept ready
for this very hour and day and month and year
were released to kill a third of mankind.

———

REVELATION 9:15

heir power is indeed staggering to behold. The force of the angels in unleashing destruction and violence is especially evident in Revelation as Christ opens the seven seals.

O Lord God of Hosts, who is like you?
You are mighty, O Lord,
and your faithfulness surrounds you.

———

PSALM 89:8

But powerful as angels are, they are not all-powerful like God. They have no force of their own, and are impotent without God. They can exercise only the energy God channels through them. Angels would have no power if it were not given them from above.

He who did not spare his own Son,
but gave him up for us all —
how will he not also, along with him,
graciously give us all things?

———

ROMANS 8:32

Surely "all things" must include angels.... Today, do angels still do all that the Bible shows them doing in the past? I see no biblical reason why they cannot and will not, because God has not changed. He still communicates. He is near to us. He is our Savior and our loving Father.

Still another angel, who had charge of the fire,
came from the altar . . ..

———

REVELATION 14:18

We associate fire with hell, and frequently think of flames as the devil's instrument. But hell is set afire by God and his angels, who will toss both Satan and all who belong to him into the torturing flames of "the lake of burning sulfur" (Revelation 20:10,15). Fire is God's tool, and he makes it the property of angels.

There before me was a man dressed in linen,
with a belt of the finest gold around his waist.
His body was like chrysolite, his face like lightning,
his eyes like flaming torches,
his arms and legs like the gleam of burnished bronze,
and his voice like the sound of a multitude.

———

DANIEL 10:5-7

Daniel was certain about what he saw. His report of the awesome figure he saw on the riverbank has been called Scripture's most detailed description of an angel's appearance.

There before me was a white horse,
whose rider is called Faithful and True. With justice he judges
and makes war. . . .
The armies of heaven were following him,
riding on white horses and dressed in fine linen,
white and clean.

REVELATION 19:11-14

The color white in Scripture is associated not only with purity but also with joy. The whiteness gets even more dazzling as we picture the Lord's ride to final victory with his angels. Pure, snow-white joy is what awaits us as we share in the pure, snow-white victory of the Lord and his angels.

Elisha prayed, "O Lord, open his eyes so he may see." Then the Lord opened the servant's eyes, and he looked and saw the hills full of horses and chariots of fire all around Elisha.

———

2 KINGS 6:17

There must be quite a lot of intervening angels around that we just never notice — but sometimes, when the time is right, God takes the scales off our eyes so we can see them.

Another mighty angel
gave a loud shout like the roar of a lion.
When he shouted, the voices
of the seven thunders spoke.

———————

REVELATION 10:1-3

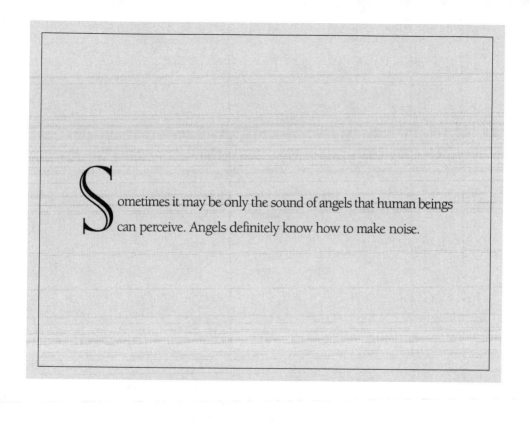

Sometimes it may be only the sound of angels that human beings can perceive. Angels definitely know how to make noise.

Lift your eyes and look to the heavens:
Who created all these?
He who brings out the starry host one by one,
and calls them each by name.
Because of his great power and mighty strength,
not one of them is missing.

———

ISAIAH 40:26

The clear night sky may be one of our best pictures right now of the host of angels arrayed like stars around God's throne-room, radiating praise and worship. Go outside some night soon, and put your focus in that direction, especially if earthly concerns and difficulties are weighing you down.

The word of the Lord came to Abram in a vision . . . .
He took him outside and said,
"Look up at the heavens and count the stars—
if indeed you can count them."

———

GENESIS 15:1-5

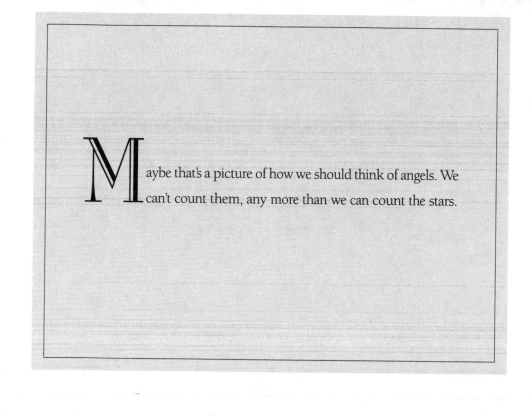

aybe that's a picture of how we should think of angels. We can't count them, any more than we can count the stars.

When I consider your heavens,
the work of your fingers,
the moon and the stars, which you have set in place,
what is man that you are mindful of him...?
You made him a little lower
than the heavenly beings.

———

PSALM 8:3-5

David had his mind on man, even as he gazed at the star-host shining from horizon to horizon. They made him think of angels — heavenly beings who were above him like the stars, and yet not so very far. Like David, we can see in those stars an amazing picture of God's care and concern for us. It's a love coming through not only by way of thousands or millions of angels whom God created to serve us, but also in a thousand or a million other ways as well.

Do everything without complaining or arguing,
so that you may become blameless and pure,
children of God without fault
in a crooked and depraved generation,
in which you shine like stars in the universe
as you hold out the word of life.

PHILIPPIANS 2:14-16

So the stars are a good reminder of angels, but also of something more. We too can be more like angels than we might have thought possible. For we, too, have been charged by the Lord Jesus with faithfully communicating his divine message — the gospel. We too can be like stars, as long as we don't let our grumbling selfishness get in the way of our testimony.

*The time came when the beggar died
and the angels carried him to Abraham's side.*

———

LUKE 16:22

I've come to believe from Scripture that angels take believers home to heaven when we die. I have to tell you honestly that this is the first time I've been really convinced of that. I had always wondered about it. But now I realize there's strong justification for believing it.

Part Three

GOD'S MESSENGERS

*I looked, and there before me was a messenger,
a holy one, coming down from heaven.*

———————

DANIEL 4:13

In the Bible, our English word "angel" translates the Hebrew word *mal'ak* in the Old Testament and the Greek word *angelos* in the New. The core meaning of both those words is *messenger.* That's the essence of who and what angels are. They are couriers for Someone other than themselves. They're Someone else's ambassadors, Someone else's agents. They represent only him, and never themselves.

Praise the Lord, you his angels,
you mighty ones who do his bidding,
who obey his word.
Praise the Lord, all his heavenly hosts,
you his servants who do his will.

———

PSALM 103:20-21

Apart from God, angels can do nothing and are nothing. Their very food and drink is to do his will and accomplish his work. And God's will and work for angels is to *communicate his messages,* both by what they say and what they do.

While I was still in prayer,
Gabriel . . . came to me in swift flight
about the time of the evening sacrifice.
He instructed me and said to me,
"Daniel, I have now come to give you
insight and understanding. . . ."

———————

DANIEL 9:21-22

They are *his* messengers. When they give us strength or enlightenment, it is God's strength or enlightenment that they impart. Their encouragement is God's encouragement. Their guidance is God's guidance. Their protection is God's protection. When they bring comfort, it is God's comfort they offer. And when they bring wrath, it is God's wrath they inflict.

Last night an angel of the God whose I am
and whom I serve stood beside me and said,
"Do not be afraid, Paul. . . . God has graciously
given you the lives of all who sail with you."

———————

ACTS 27:23-24

Angels are just a means of communication from the God who communicates. Through what angels say and do, God personally expresses his friendship to us and his fatherhood and much more. What's important is the message angels bring — not the messengers themselves.

Jesus said to him, "Away from me, Satan!
For it is written: 'Worship the Lord your God,
and serve him only.'" Then the devil left him,
and angels came and attended him.

MATTHEW 4:10-11

Our Master's body and face are thin from forty days of fasting. His skin is darkened by the sun. Now, coming in visible form — just as the devil came — a group of angels appear at the side of Jesus. They kneel before him and reach out to him with food…. Angels are great comforters and servants, bringing encouragement and strength in their hands and in their voices.

But we see Jesus,
who was made a little lower than the angels,
now crowned with glory and honor because he suffered death,
so that by the grace of God he might
taste death for everyone.

———

HEBREWS 2:9

Christ's mediation brings us what any mediation of angels could never begin to accomplish: the freedom and eternal salvation of our souls. That's why in the New Testament the mention of angels is so completely dominated by a focus on the excellence of Christ in every way.

During the night an angel of the Lord opened
the doors of the jail and brought them out.
"Go, stand in the temple courts," he said, "and tell
the people the full message of this new life."

———————

ACTS 5:19-20

Angels are always one-way messengers. They are God's messengers to us, and never our messengers to God. No one in Scripture ever prays to an angel, and neither should we. They are not go-betweens or mediators between us and heaven.

Then the angel said to me,
"... I am a fellow servant with you
and with your brothers who hold
to the testimony of Jesus."

———

REVELATION 19:9-10

When the apostle John wanted to worship an angel, the point the angel made in his reply (after telling John, "No, don't do it!") was how alike he and John were. The angel was God's servant, just as John and the prophets were God's servants, and just as all of us are God's servants when we speak a word of testimony for his sake and on his behalf.

Suddenly two men in clothes that gleamed like lightning stood beside them. . . . The men said to them, "Why do you look for the living among the dead? He is not here; he has risen! Remember how he told you . . . ."

LUKE 20:35-36

These angels certainly have their wits about them. They don't just have personality — they've got class and style, even while they're being direct and businesslike. I'm guessing that in heaven, you and I will be something like them.

Part Four

HOLY
WORSHIPERS

I fell down to worship at the feet of the angel. . . .
But he said to me, "Do not do it! . . . .
Worship God!"

————————

REVELATION 22:8-9

We too are spiritual beings, and as we go honestly and carefully into a deeper study of angels, our spirits cannot help but experience the desire to worship. So as we go on, if you remember any words at all that you've heard angels speak in Scripture, remember especially these two: *Worship God!*

You shall have no other gods before me.
You shall not make for yourself an idol
in the form of anything in heaven above . . . .

EXODUS 20:3-4

Most of us find John's fall into angel-worship quite understandable. Who would not be tempted to fall down before these majestic beings?... We're tempted enough as it is to worship the work of our own hands. What would we do if we saw angels every day?

Do not let anyone who delights in . . . the worship of angels disqualify you for the prize.

COLOSSIANS 2:18

Angels must never receive our worship. Scripture hits this one head-on.... Worshiping angels is another exhibition of the basic idolatry charged against sinful mankind in Romans 1:25 — "They exchanged the truth of God for a lie, and worshiped and served created things rather than the Creator."

Set your hearts on things above,
where Christ is seated at the right hand of God.
Set your minds on things above,
not on earthly things.

———

COLOSSIANS 3:1-2

When Paul tells us to set our minds and hearts on things above, he points out specifically that heaven is where Christ is. Angels are there too, but Paul doesn't put them in the spotlight. It's Christ who can make us heavenly minded, not angels.

Praise the Lord from the heavens,
praise him in the heights above.
Praise him, all his angels,
praise him, all his heavenly hosts.

———————

PSALM 148:1-2

salm 148 begins by calling on everything in the heavens and the heights above to give God praise. The angels are continually and joyfully meeting this requirement of praise.

The Lord came from Sinai
and dawned over them . . . .
He came with myriads of holy ones . . . .

———————

DEUTERONOMY 33:2

oth *myriad* and *holy ones* are words often used in the Bible in connection with angels. *Myriad* can mean ten thousand or simply an exceedingly vast number, and *holy ones* reflects the purity of the angels' devotion to God.

...that at the name of Jesus
every knee should bow, in heaven and on earth
and under the earth.

PHILIPPIANS 2:1

Angels, men, and demons must all alike bend the knee some day to acknowledge the glory and supremacy of Jesus. Have you done so today?

When God brings
his firstborn into the world, he says,
"Let all God's angels worship him."

———————

HEBREWS 1:6

The most extensive treatment of angels in the entire Bible stretches over the first two chapters in the book of Hebrews. But the whole discussion makes one resounding point — Christ is utterly superior to angels.

He appeared in a body...
was seen by angels....

———————

1 TIMOTHY 3:16

Jesus left heaven, the home of spirits, and came to earth, the home of flesh. And angels watched in wonder.

Since the children have flesh and blood,
he too shared in their humanity so that by his death
he might destroy him who holds
the power of death — that is, the devil. . . .
For surely it is not angels he helps,
but Abraham's descendants.

HEBREWS 2:14-16

As spirits, angels cannot bleed or die. Christ could, and did — for you and for me. And for you and for me, it's that distinction between Christ and angels that makes an eternity of difference. For by it, Christ was able "to destroy him who holds the power of death — that is, the devil"

I tell you the truth, you shall see heaven open,
and the angels of God ascending and
descending on the Son of Man.

———————

JOHN 1:51

Even now angels may come and go between heaven and earth only by way of Christ. Solely in obedience to his will are they sent to serve us. His own ministry to us, his plans for us, and his protection of us are the busy stairway they use in their daily diligence of attending to our needs.

The prophets . . . spoke of the things that have now been told you by those who have preached the gospel to you by the Holy Spirit sent from heaven. Even angels long to look into these things.

———

1 PETER 1:11-12

God sent his Son to be born into human flesh and to take upon himself all the curse and the death and the doom that was ours. And what do the angels think about all this? The apostle Peter tells us they are gripped with an abiding curiosity about it. And I suppose they always will be.

I tell you,
there is rejoicing in the presence of the angels of God
over one sinner who repents.

LUKE 15:10

Angels, likewise, can't fully imagine what's it's like to be in my condition. Redemption for them is not a personal reality to enjoy. But they can be excited about it on my behalf.

His intent was that now, through the church,
the manifold wisdom of God should be
made known to the rulers and authorities
in the heavenly realms.

———————

EPHESIANS 3:10

God is showing something to the angels! And that something is his wisdom on display in the Church — in us! We are the stage where God's new production is performed before a heavenly audience. We are the showroom where his latest masterpiece is unveiled to angelic applause. We are the arena where his matchless feats of skill are exhibited to the sound of angel cheers.

*But even if we or an angel from heaven
should preach a gospel other than
the one we preached to you,
let him be eternally condemned!*

———

GALATIANS 1:8

Absolutely everything is at stake in our answer to the good news. To be right with God through Christ is heaven; by comparison, to be right only with an angel is hell.

*And they sang a new song: "You are worthy
to take the scroll and to open its seals,
because you were slain, and with your blood
you purchased men for God from every tribe
and language and people and nation."*

REVELATION 5:9

Here in the high places which have always been their home, the angels' praise centers on this: the entrance into God's holy heaven of those who don't deserve to be there, all through the blood of the murdered Son of God.

But you have come to Mount Zion,
to the heavenly Jerusalem,
the city of the living God. You have come
to thousands upon thousands of angels
in joyful assembly.

———————

HEBREWS 12:22

There's a sense in which we're already in the presence of angels. That's part of the eternal picture we're to look at now. Not only have we come to God, and to Jesus, and to "the sprinkled blood that speaks a better word than the blood of Abel" — but we've also come to all those happy angels. In our heart of hearts, in our deepest thoughts, we can be there — now.

The four living creatures
and the twenty-four elders fell down before the Lamb.
Each one had a harp and they were holding
golden bowls full of incense,
which are the prayers of the saints.

REVELATION 5:8

What precious prayers from you have gone up today to help fill those bowls as they rest in the holy hands of angels? Have you prayed today for God's kingdom to come? Have you prayed for his kingdom to be born in the lives of your family and friends and neighbors whom you love, but who are not yet believers? Have you prayed for his will to be done in your life, just as it's already done by the angels in heaven?

All the angels were standing around the throne
and around the elders and the four living creatures.
They fell down on their faces before the throne
and worshiped God.

———

REVELATION 7:11

From all we can tell in Scripture, these spirit beings right now are worshiping in this very manner the same God whom you and I claim as our Lord. If these holy creatures, awesome as they are, cry out in praise of his holiness day and night, how much should we? If they who are pure and splendid fall down before God again and again, how often should we?

Wherever the spirit would go, they would go . . . .
The creatures sped back and forth
like flashes of lightning.

———

EZEKIEL 1:12-14

Although angels are so perfect in their fear of God, we don't sense at all that they're frozen in fear. Instead they show great freedom in their worship. They're free to worship God the way he wants to be worshiped.

This last scene fades.

Our guide puts forth the same question he asked us in our earlier trip:

"What have you learned?"

After a pause, you decide to answer for both of us:

"That angels truly love the Lord, and will always love to serve him...

and so will I."